Life After Divorce

Tawanda Tawanda

Published by Tawanda Tawanda, 2024.

Life After Dirvoce

Introduction: A New Chapter Begins

Divorce is one of the most painful experiences a person can endure. It's a tearing apart of what was once whole, leaving behind wounds that can feel impossible to heal. You may be wrestling with feelings of failure, shame, anger, grief, or even fear of what the future holds. You're not alone in this journey, and more importantly, you're not without hope.

The Bible reminds us that God is near to the brokenhearted (Psalm 34:18). He doesn't abandon us in our pain, nor does He leave us to navigate the aftermath of divorce on our own. Instead, He walks alongside us, offering healing, guidance, and the promise of new beginnings. This book is rooted in that truth—a guide to help you move forward, not in isolation but with God as your foundation.

Whether you are freshly divorced, still reeling from the pain years later, or somewhere in between, this book is for you. It's not about placing blame, reliving the past, or pretending the hurt doesn't exist. Instead, it's about finding a path toward healing, rediscovering your identity in Christ, and embracing the future God has planned for you.

Life after divorce isn't the end—it's the beginning of a new chapter. While it may not be the story you originally envisioned, it can still be a beautiful testimony of God's redemptive power. He specializes in bringing beauty from ashes and turning mourning into joy (Isaiah 61:3).

Together, we'll explore how to navigate this season biblically, focusing on what truly matters: faith, forgiveness, rebuilding, and embracing God's purpose for your life. This journey won't always be easy, but it will be worth it. Because with God, nothing is wasted—not even the heartbreak of divorce.

Take a deep breath. You're stepping into something new, and you don't have to do it alone. God is with you, and He has a plan to bring hope, healing, and renewal. Let's walk this road together, one step at a time, trusting Him to lead the way.

Chapter 1: Facing the Pain and Finding Peace

Divorce is often described as a kind of death—the death of a marriage, dreams, and the life you once knew. It leaves behind a trail of emotional turmoil that can feel overwhelming. From heartbreak and anger to confusion and guilt, the pain of divorce is deeply personal, and no two journeys are the same.

Acknowledging this pain is the first step toward healing. Often, society encourages us to move on quickly or to suppress our emotions, but Scripture tells us that it's okay to grieve. The Bible is filled with examples of godly men and women pouring out their sorrows to God, and His response is always one of compassion and understanding. As Psalm 34:18 reminds us, "The Lord is close to the brokenhearted and saves those who are crushed in spirit."

—-

Grieving the Loss

Grieving after divorce is not only natural but necessary. You may find yourself mourning not just the relationship but also the future you had envisioned. It's important to let yourself feel these emotions without judgment. Trying to suppress them or rush through them can lead to prolonged pain and unresolved wounds.

What Grief Looks Like:

Grief after divorce may manifest as sadness, anger, denial, or even relief. Some days, you may feel like you're making progress, only to be overwhelmed by sorrow the next. Remember that grief isn't linear; it's a process.

Biblical Perspective on Grief:

Scripture doesn't shy away from acknowledging pain. Jesus Himself wept over the loss of a friend (John 11:35), and King David poured out his anguish in the Psalms. These examples show us that it's not only acceptable to grieve but that God welcomes us to bring our pain to Him.

—-

The Danger of Staying in Despair

While grieving is essential, it's equally important not to remain in despair indefinitely. Prolonged sorrow can lead to bitterness, hopelessness, and isolation. The enemy thrives in these moments, whispering lies that you are unworthy, unloved, or irreparably broken.

However, God's Word is a powerful weapon against despair. He promises to be near to those who are brokenhearted and to bring beauty from ashes (Isaiah 61:3). This doesn't mean the pain will disappear overnight, but it does mean there is hope for healing.

—-

Practical Steps to Begin Healing

Healing is a journey, and every journey requires intentional steps. Here are some biblically inspired practices to help you face the pain and move toward peace:

1. Journaling Your Emotions

Writing can be a powerful tool for processing emotions. Use a journal to pour out your thoughts, fears, and frustrations. This practice not only helps you understand your feelings but also allows you to see patterns and progress over time.

Start with Prayer: Begin each journaling session with a prayer, inviting God to guide your thoughts.

Focus on Honesty: Don't censor yourself. God knows your heart and can handle your raw emotions.

2. Seeking Support

God designed us for community, and walking through divorce is not something you should do alone. Seek out trusted friends, family members, or a counselor who can offer wisdom, encouragement, and accountability.

Christian Counseling: A counselor with a biblical perspective can help you navigate the emotional and spiritual challenges of divorce.

Faith Communities: Joining a divorce recovery group or small Bible study can provide a sense of belonging and shared understanding.

3. Practicing Prayerful Surrender

Letting go of the past and trusting God with your future is perhaps the most challenging yet transformative step. Prayerful surrender means releasing control and allowing God to work in your heart and circumstances.

Daily Surrender: Begin each day by laying your burdens at God's feet. Pray for strength, wisdom, and peace.

Meditate on Scripture: Choose verses that remind you of God's faithfulness and repeat them throughout the day. For example, "Cast all your anxiety on Him because He cares for you." (1 Peter 5:7)

—

Finding Peace in God's Presence

True peace doesn't come from the absence of pain but from the presence of God. Spending time in His Word, worshiping, and meditating on His promises can provide a deep sense of comfort and reassurance.

Worship as Healing: Even when it feels difficult, worship can shift your focus from your pain to God's power. Songs of praise remind us of His sovereignty and goodness.

Scripture for Comfort:

"Come to me, all you who are weary and burdened, and I will give you rest." (Matthew 11:28)

"He heals the brokenhearted and binds up their wounds." (Psalm 147:3)

—-

A Closing Reflection

Facing the pain of divorce is not about ignoring or minimizing it—it's about bringing it before the Lord and allowing Him to transform it. As you take these first steps, remember that healing is a process. Be patient with yourself and trust in God's timing.

As you move forward, hold onto this truth: God's love for you has not changed. He sees your pain, hears your cries, and is working behind the scenes to bring you to a place of peace. Take heart—this is not the end of your story, but the beginning of a new chapter, written by the Author of life Himself.

—-

Would you like to add personal stories or examples to this chapter?

Chapter 2: Rediscovering Your Identity in Christ

Divorce can leave you questioning everything—your worth, purpose, and identity. For many, the relationship they were in became a part of their self-definition. When that relationship ends, it can feel like losing a piece of yourself. But while your marital status may have changed, one thing has not: your identity as a child of God.

God created you intentionally, with love, and in His image. Your worth isn't defined by your circumstances or by another person's actions; it is rooted in who you are in Christ. Rediscovering this truth is a vital step in your journey of healing and renewal.

—-

Understanding Identity Through God's Eyes

At the heart of rediscovering yourself is embracing your identity as someone made in God's image. Genesis 1:27 reminds us, "So God created mankind in his own image, in the image of God he created them; male and female he created them." This means your value is inherent and unchanging.

Divorce may have left you feeling unworthy, rejected, or broken, but these are lies the enemy uses to keep you in a place of despair. God's truth says you are:

Loved: "I have loved you with an everlasting love." (Jeremiah 31:3)

Chosen: "You are a chosen people, a royal priesthood, a holy nation, God's special possession." (1 Peter 2:9)

Valuable: "Are not five sparrows sold for two pennies? Yet not one of them is forgotten by God. Indeed, the very hairs of your head are all numbered. Don't be afraid; you are worth more than many sparrows." (Luke 12:6-7)

Your identity in Christ is unshakable, no matter the challenges you face.

—-

Shedding False Labels

Divorce often comes with a barrage of labels: "failure," "unworthy," "unlovable." These labels can cloud your understanding of who you truly are. It's essential to shed these false labels and replace them with the truth of God's Word.

Activity: Identifying Labels

1. Take a piece of paper and draw two columns.

2. In the left column, write down the negative labels or beliefs you've internalized since your divorce (e.g., "I'm not good enough," "I'm broken").

3. In the right column, write a truth from Scripture that counters each label (e.g., "I am fearfully and wonderfully made" - Psalm 139:14).

Prayer for Renewal:

Ask God to help you see yourself as He sees you. Pray for the courage to release the lies and embrace His truth.

—-

Discovering Your Core Strengths

Divorce can make you feel like you've lost your footing, but it also presents an opportunity to rediscover your God-given strengths and gifts. Reflecting on your talents, passions, and past accomplishments can help you see the unique ways God has equipped you.

Reflection Questions:

1. What are some skills or abilities I've relied on in difficult times?

2. What activities bring me joy or a sense of purpose?

3. How have others described my strengths or admired qualities in me?

Activity: Strength Inventory

Write down at least five strengths or gifts you believe God has given you. If you struggle to identify them, ask a trusted friend or family member to help. Then, reflect on how these strengths can be used for God's glory in this new season of life.

—-

Affirmations Rooted in Scripture

Words have power. Speaking truth over yourself can help reframe your thoughts and align your perspective with God's Word.

Daily Affirmations:

Use these affirmations to remind yourself of your identity in Christ:

1. "I am created in God's image and deeply loved." (Genesis 1:27, John 3:16)

2. "I am forgiven and redeemed by His grace." (Ephesians 1:7)

3. "I am fearfully and wonderfully made." (Psalm 139:14)

4. "God has a plan and purpose for my life." (Jeremiah 29:11)

Activity: Personalizing Scripture

Choose one verse that speaks to you and rewrite it as a personal declaration. For example, turn Romans 8:37 into: "I am more than a conqueror through Him who loves me."

—-

Rebuilding Confidence in Christ

Rediscovering your identity involves rebuilding your confidence—not in yourself alone, but in who you are through Christ. When you trust in God's power and promises, you can step into this new chapter with courage and hope.

Key Practices for Confidence:

1. Regular Prayer and Meditation: Spend time in God's presence, asking Him to renew your mind and fill you with His peace.

2. Surround Yourself with Encouragement: Seek out people who remind you of your worth and point you to Christ.

3. Take Small Steps: Confidence grows with action. Whether it's starting a new hobby, volunteering, or pursuing a career goal, stepping outside your comfort zone can help you rediscover your potential.

—

Living as God's Masterpiece

Ephesians 2:10 declares, "For we are God's handiwork, created in Christ Jesus to do good works, which God prepared in advance for us to do." You are not an accident or an afterthought. You are God's masterpiece, uniquely designed for His purpose.

Divorce may feel like a detour, but it doesn't disqualify you from God's plan. In fact, your experiences can become a testimony of His grace and redemption. As you rediscover your identity, remember that you are loved, chosen, and equipped for the good works He has prepared for you.

—

A Closing Exercise

Take a moment to sit quietly with God. Ask Him to reveal who you are in His eyes. Write down any words, phrases, or Scriptures that come to mind. Keep this list somewhere visible as a reminder of your true identity.

Rediscovering your identity in Christ is not a one-time event but a journey of continual growth. Each day, as you lean into His truth, you will uncover more of the person He created you to be. You are His, and that is enough.

—

Would you like additional reflection questions or specific examples for this chapter?

Chapter 3: Rebuilding Your Faith Foundation

When life feels shattered by divorce, the most crucial foundation you can rely on is your faith in God. While relationships with others may falter, God remains steadfast. Scripture reminds us, "The Lord is my rock, my fortress, and my deliverer" (Psalm 18:2). In this challenging season, leaning on Him can provide the strength, peace, and direction you need to rebuild your life.

This chapter focuses on how to rebuild and deepen your faith foundation, allowing God to restore your spirit and renew your hope.

—-

Why Faith Matters After Divorce

Divorce often leaves people feeling untethered. The routines, relationships, and shared dreams that once provided a sense of stability are suddenly gone. In these moments of uncertainty, faith becomes your anchor.

Faith Provides Stability: Just as a house needs a strong foundation to withstand storms, your life needs a solid spiritual base to endure challenges.

Faith Renews Perspective: When pain clouds your vision, faith helps you see that God is still in control and working all things together for good (Romans 8:28).

Faith Brings Healing: God is not only a fortress but also a healer. He binds up the wounds of the brokenhearted (Psalm 147:3).

Rebuilding your faith isn't about pretending everything is fine. It's about coming to God with your doubts, fears, and brokenness, trusting Him to restore and guide you.

—-

1. Establishing a Consistent Prayer Life

Prayer is one of the most powerful ways to connect with God. It's not just about asking for things but about building a relationship with your Creator.

Why Prayer Matters:

Prayer invites God into your pain and allows Him to work in your heart. It provides comfort, guidance, and clarity. Even when words fail, the Holy Spirit intercedes on your behalf (Romans 8:26).

Practical Steps to Build a Prayer Routine:

1. Set Aside Time Daily: Start with just five to ten minutes each day. Choose a quiet place where you can focus.

2. Be Honest with God: Share your emotions openly. If you're angry, hurt, or confused, tell Him. He can handle your honesty.

3. Incorporate Gratitude: Thank God for His presence and for small blessings, even in the midst of pain. Gratitude shifts your perspective.

4. Use Scripture in Prayer: Praying God's Word is powerful. For example, declare Psalm 18:2 over your life: "Lord, be my rock, fortress, and deliverer in this time of need."

Activity: Creating a Prayer Journal

Write down your prayers and the ways God answers them. Over time, this journal will become a testimony of His faithfulness.

—-

2. Diving Deeper into the Bible

God's Word is a source of wisdom, encouragement, and healing. After divorce, it can serve as a guide to help you navigate this new season.

Benefits of Engaging with Scripture:

It reminds you of God's promises.

It offers wisdom for making decisions.

It strengthens your faith and renews your mind (Romans 12:2).

Ways to Study the Bible:

1. Start with Psalms and Proverbs: The Psalms provide comfort and express raw emotion, while Proverbs offers practical wisdom for daily living.

2. Use Devotional Guides: Choose a divorce recovery devotional or one focused on healing and hope.

3. Memorize Key Verses: Internalizing Scripture helps you draw on God's truth throughout your day. Examples include:

"The Lord is near to all who call on Him." (Psalm 145:18)

"He will cover you with His feathers, and under His wings you will find refuge." (Psalm 91:4)

Activity: The SOAP Bible Study Method

S (Scripture): Write out a verse that stands out to you.

O (Observation): Reflect on what the verse means in context.

A (Application): Consider how it applies to your life right now.

P (Prayer): Pray the verse back to God, asking Him to help you live it out.

—-

3. Surrounding Yourself with a Faith Community

Healing is not a journey to take alone. God created us for community, and being around others who share your faith can provide encouragement and accountability.

Benefits of Faith-Based Relationships:

Encouragement during tough times.

Wisdom from others who have experienced similar struggles.

A sense of belonging and purpose.

How to Find a Faith Community:

1. Join a Small Group: Many churches offer groups for divorce recovery or general Bible studies.

2. Attend Church Regularly: Worshiping alongside others strengthens your connection to the body of Christ.

3. Volunteer: Serving in church ministries can help you build meaningful connections and rediscover your purpose.

Activity: Building Supportive Relationships

Make a list of people or groups who can support you spiritually. Reach out to at least one person this week to share your journey and ask for prayer.

—-

Trusting God to Rebuild

Rebuilding your faith foundation doesn't happen overnight, but each small step brings you closer to God and His plans for your life. He is the ultimate restorer. As Isaiah 61:3 promises, He gives "a crown of beauty instead of ashes, the oil of joy instead of mourning, and a garment of praise instead of a spirit of despair."

Be Patient with Yourself: There will be days when your faith feels strong and days when doubt creeps in. Both are part of the journey.

Celebrate Progress: Every prayer, every verse read, and every connection made is a step forward.

—-

A Closing Prayer

Heavenly Father, thank You for being my rock and fortress during this season of rebuilding. Help me to draw closer to You, trusting in Your promises and Your plans for my life. Strengthen my faith, guide me in Your Word, and surround me with a community of believers who will uplift me. Lord, I surrender my pain and my future into Your hands. Thank You for being my deliverer and my constant source of hope. In Jesus' name, Amen.

As you strengthen your relationship with God, remember that He is the foundation on which you can rebuild a life of purpose, peace, and joy. Keep seeking Him, and you will find all that you need to move forward.

—

Would you like to add more personal testimonies or stories of faith in this chapter?

Chapter 4: Forgiveness: The Key to Freedom

Forgiveness is one of the most challenging aspects of healing after a divorce. The pain caused by betrayal, unmet expectations, or unkind actions can feel overwhelming. Yet, forgiveness is not only a command from God but also a gift to yourself. It frees you from the chains of bitterness and allows you to move forward with peace.

As Colossians 3:13 reminds us, "Bear with each other and forgive one another if any of you has a grievance against someone. Forgive as the Lord forgave you." The forgiveness we extend to others mirrors the grace God has already shown us. This chapter explores why forgiveness is essential, how to navigate the process, and how it can lead to true freedom.

—-

Why Forgiveness Matters

Forgiveness Brings Freedom: Holding onto anger or resentment keeps you emotionally tied to the person who hurt you. Forgiveness severs that tie, giving you the freedom to focus on your healing and future.

Forgiveness Reflects God's Grace: God has forgiven us for our sins through Christ. As recipients of His grace, we are called to extend that same grace to others, even when it's difficult.

Forgiveness Heals Your Heart: Studies show that forgiveness reduces stress, improves mental health, and fosters inner peace. Spiritually, it allows God to work fully in your life.

It's important to note that forgiveness does not mean condoning harmful behavior, forgetting the past, or reconciling with someone who hasn't changed. It's a personal decision to release the burden of resentment and entrust justice to God.

—-

1. Forgiving Your Ex-Spouse

Forgiving your ex-spouse may feel impossible, especially if their actions caused deep wounds. However, forgiveness is not about excusing their behavior; it's about freeing yourself from the grip of bitterness.

Recognize Their Humanity: Everyone is flawed and makes mistakes. While their actions may have been hurtful, they are still a person created in God's image.

Entrust Justice to God: Romans 12:19 reminds us, "Do not take revenge, my dear friends, but leave room for God's wrath, for it is written: 'It is mine to avenge; I will repay,' says the Lord." Trust that God will handle justice in His perfect way and timing.

Pray for Them: This may feel counterintuitive, but praying for your ex-spouse can soften your heart and align your perspective with God's.

—-

2. Forgiving Yourself

After divorce, self-forgiveness is often the hardest to achieve. Whether you feel guilt for things you did or regret for decisions you didn't make, it's easy to get stuck in a cycle of self-blame.

Accept God's Forgiveness: If you've confessed your sins to God, He has forgiven you (1 John 1:9). Holding onto guilt after receiving His grace denies the power of the cross.

Speak Truth Over Yourself: Replace negative self-talk with affirmations of God's love and forgiveness. For example, declare, "I am redeemed by His grace" (Ephesians 1:7).

Learn from the Past: Instead of dwelling on mistakes, use them as lessons for growth. Ask God to show you how He can bring good from your experiences.

---

3. Forgiving Others Involved

Sometimes, people outside the marriage—such as friends, family, or in-laws—play a role in the pain of divorce. Forgiveness must extend to anyone who contributed to your hurt.

Recognize the Ripple Effect: Divorce impacts everyone differently, and others' actions may have been misguided attempts to cope.

Set Boundaries if Necessary: Forgiveness doesn't mean allowing someone to continue harmful behavior. You can forgive while establishing healthy boundaries.

Let Go for Your Sake: Harboring anger toward others only prolongs your pain. Release it to God and focus on your own healing.

Practical Steps Toward Forgiveness

1. Guided Prayers for Forgiveness

Prayer invites God into your healing process and helps you surrender your pain to Him. Use the following prayer as a guide:

"Heavenly Father, I come before You with the pain and anger I feel toward [person's name]. I confess my struggle to forgive and ask for Your help. Lord, soften my heart and remind me of the grace You have shown me. I choose to release [person's name] to You and trust that You will handle justice. Bring healing to my heart and peace to my mind. In Jesus' name, Amen."

2. Recognize the Benefits of Letting Go

Write down the benefits of forgiveness in your journal. These might include emotional freedom, spiritual growth, and improved relationships. Reflect on how holding onto resentment affects your life versus how forgiveness can bring peace.

3. Journaling Letters of Release

Writing a letter to the person you need to forgive is a powerful way to process your emotions and release your pain. You don't need to send the letter; the purpose is to express your feelings and let them go.

Start by addressing the person directly.

Describe the hurt they caused and how it made you feel.

End with a declaration of forgiveness: "I choose to forgive you and release this pain to God."

4. Daily Affirmations of Forgiveness

Remind yourself daily of your commitment to forgive. For example:

"I forgive others as God has forgiven me."

"I release my pain to God and embrace His peace."

—-

The Journey of Forgiveness

Forgiveness is not a one-time event but a journey. You may find yourself revisiting painful memories or struggling with anger long after you've chosen to forgive. That's okay. Each time, bring those feelings to God and reaffirm your decision to let go.

Be Patient with Yourself: Healing takes time, and so does forgiveness. Celebrate small victories along the way.

Seek Support: Share your journey with a trusted friend, counselor, or pastor who can offer encouragement and prayer.

—-

Forgiveness Brings Healing

When you forgive, you create space for God's healing work in your life. The pain doesn't disappear instantly, but as you release your hurt, you make room for His peace, joy, and restoration.

As you reflect on forgiveness, remember Jesus' ultimate example on the cross. In His moment of greatest pain, He said, "Father, forgive them, for they do not know what they are doing" (Luke 23:34). If Christ can extend such grace, He can also empower you to forgive those who have hurt you.

—-

A Closing Reflection

Take a moment to sit with God and reflect on these questions:

Who do I need to forgive?

What steps can I take this week to move toward forgiveness?

How has God's forgiveness changed my life?

As you work through these questions, remember that forgiveness is not about erasing the past but about freeing your future. Trust God to guide you, and He will replace bitterness with His peace.

Would you like to include personal testimonies or examples in this chapter?

Chapter 5: Navigating Loneliness and Building Community

Divorce often brings a profound sense of loneliness. The absence of a spouse, the shift in routines, and changes in social circles can leave you feeling isolated. However, God never intended for us to face life alone. As Psalm 68:6 reminds us, "God sets the lonely in families." He places us within communities to provide love, support, and a sense of belonging.

In this chapter, we'll explore practical ways to navigate loneliness, rediscover meaningful relationships, and build a strong support network rooted in faith.

—-

Understanding Loneliness After Divorce

Loneliness after divorce can stem from:

Physical Separation: Sharing your life with someone and suddenly being alone creates a noticeable void.

Emotional Disconnection: Divorce often strains or severs other relationships, leaving you feeling misunderstood or unsupported.

Social Changes: Friends may take sides, or you may lose mutual friendships, further isolating you.

Loneliness is a natural part of the healing process, but it doesn't have to define this season of your life. Instead, it can be an opportunity to deepen your connection with God and forge new, healthy relationships.

—-

1. Embracing God's Presence in Your Loneliness

Before building connections with others, it's essential to lean into your relationship with God. He is always present, even in your loneliest moments.

Seek His Comfort: Pour out your heart to God through prayer. Psalm 34:18 assures us, "The Lord is close to the brokenhearted and saves those who are crushed in spirit."

Find Solace in His Word: Scriptures like Isaiah 41:10 ("Do not fear, for I am with you") remind us of God's unwavering presence.

Cultivate Quiet Moments with Him: Use this time of solitude to worship, meditate, and grow closer to God.

When you anchor yourself in God's love, you'll feel less alone, even in moments of solitude.

—-

2. Joining Faith-Based Communities

God often works through people to bring comfort and encouragement. Being part of a faith community can provide the support and companionship you need during this time.

Join Small Groups: Many churches offer small groups for specific life stages, including divorce recovery. These groups provide a safe space to share your journey, study God's Word, and build friendships with others who understand your experience.

Participate in Bible Studies: Engaging in a study deepens your faith while connecting you with like-minded believers.

Volunteer in Church Ministries: Serving in areas like outreach, children's ministry, or worship teams allows you to form bonds with others while making a positive impact.

Activity: Research local churches or ministries offering small groups or volunteer opportunities. Attend at least one gathering this month and make an effort to connect with someone new.

—-

3. Cultivating Healthy Relationships

Divorce often brings significant relational shifts. It's an opportunity to evaluate existing connections and cultivate new ones that are nurturing and uplifting.

Rebuild Family Connections: Divorce can strain family relationships, but it's also an opportunity to strengthen bonds with parents, siblings, or extended family.

Spend quality time together.

Share your journey honestly, and allow them to support you.

Pray together for healing and unity.

Reconnect with Old Friends: Reach out to friends you may have drifted from. Authentic friendships often stand the test of time, even after seasons of separation.

Set Boundaries: Avoid relationships that pull you away from God or your healing process. Surround yourself with people who uplift and encourage you.

—-

4. Finding Purpose Through Service

One of the most effective ways to combat loneliness is to focus outward by helping others. Serving not only brings joy to others but also fosters a sense of belonging and purpose in your own life.

Volunteer Opportunities:

Serve at a local food bank or homeless shelter.

Participate in mission trips or outreach programs through your church.

Offer your skills (e.g., teaching, mentoring, or organizing) to benefit your community.

Activity: Write Down Your Passions: Consider what you love doing and how you can use it to serve others. For example, if you enjoy cooking, volunteer to prepare meals for church events or needy families.

By serving others, you'll often find that your own loneliness diminishes as you focus on spreading God's love.

—-

5. Building a New Vision for Community

While the relationships you had before divorce may change, this is a chance to build a new vision for your community—a group of people who support and uplift you as you move forward.

Pray for Divine Connections: Ask God to bring the right people into your life. Proverbs 27:17 reminds us, "As iron sharpens iron, so one person sharpens another."

Be Open to New Friendships: Attend events, introduce yourself to people at church, and say yes to invitations. You never know where meaningful connections may develop.

Invest in Relationships: Building strong relationships takes time and effort. Be intentional about staying in touch, offering encouragement, and creating opportunities to spend time together.

—-

Encouragement for the Journey

Loneliness is a temporary season, not a permanent state. As you lean on God, step out in faith, and invest in relationships, you'll find your life filling with love and connection again.

Remember, God has a plan for you, and He uses community to strengthen and bless His children. Allow Him to guide you toward the people and opportunities that will enrich your life and bring you closer to Him.

—-

A Closing Prayer

Heavenly Father, thank You for Your promise to set the lonely in families. In this season of loneliness, help me to feel Your presence and seek comfort in Your Word. Guide me toward the people and communities You have prepared for me. Teach me to build relationships that honor You and bring joy to my life. Thank You for being my constant companion and for surrounding me with Your love. In Jesus' name, Amen.

Would you like to expand on this chapter with personal testimonies or examples of individuals who found meaningful community after divorce?

Chapter 6: Parenting After Divorce

Parenting after divorce presents unique challenges. Balancing your role as a parent with the emotional strain of separation, navigating co-parenting dynamics, and providing stability for your children can feel overwhelming. Yet, as Proverbs 22:6 reminds us, "Start children off on the way they should go, and even when they are old they will not turn from it."

God calls parents to guide their children with love, wisdom, and biblical principles, even in difficult circumstances. This chapter explores practical strategies for effective co-parenting, creating a stable environment, and nurturing your children's spiritual growth.

—-

Understanding the Impact of Divorce on Children

Divorce affects children differently depending on their age, personality, and the circumstances surrounding the separation. Common challenges include:

Emotional Reactions: Sadness, anger, confusion, or guilt.

Behavioral Changes: Acting out, withdrawal, or declining academic performance.

Questions About Faith: Wondering why God allowed the divorce or doubting His goodness.

While these reactions are natural, your response as a parent can significantly shape their healing process.

—-

1. Prioritizing Your Children's Well-Being

Children need to feel loved, secure, and supported during this transition.

Reassure Them of Your Love: Consistently remind your children that the divorce is not their fault and that your love for them hasn't changed.

Provide Stability: Maintain routines, such as regular mealtimes, bedtimes, and family traditions. Predictability gives children a sense of security.

Be Emotionally Available: Encourage open communication. Let them express their feelings without fear of judgment or reprisal.

Activity: Set aside time each week for one-on-one moments with each child. This could be a walk, a shared hobby, or simply a time to talk.

—-

2. Navigating Co-Parenting Challenges

Effective co-parenting requires patience, communication, and a commitment to prioritize your children's needs over personal grievances.

Communicate Respectfully: Even if your relationship with your ex-spouse is strained, strive for respectful communication. Use neutral tones and keep conversations focused on the children.

Establish Clear Boundaries: Define responsibilities, schedules, and rules to reduce misunderstandings. A written co-parenting plan can help both parties stay aligned.

Model Grace: As difficult as it may be, show your children what forgiveness and grace look like. Your behavior teaches them more than words ever could.

Avoid Negative Talk: Never speak poorly of your ex-spouse in front of your children. This can create confusion and emotional distress.

Biblical Insight: Romans 12:18 says, "If it is possible, as far as it depends on you, live at peace with everyone." Strive to create a peaceful co-parenting relationship for the sake of your children.

—-

3. Maintaining Stability for Your Children

During a time of upheaval, stability becomes essential.

Stick to Consistent Rules: Agree on rules and discipline strategies with your co-parent to create a unified approach.

Provide a Safe Space: Create an environment where your children feel secure and comfortable, whether at your home or their other parent's.

Encourage Healthy Relationships: Support your children's relationship with their other parent, provided it is safe and healthy.

—-

4. Fostering Your Children's Spiritual Growth

Your children's spiritual development should remain a priority, even amidst life changes.

Pray Together: Teach your children the importance of prayer by praying with them daily for peace, wisdom, and strength.

Incorporate Devotions: Spend time reading Scripture together, using age-appropriate resources to explain God's truths.

Attend Church as a Family: Regular church attendance provides spiritual grounding and exposes your children to a supportive faith community.

Answer Faith Questions Honestly: Be prepared for your children to ask difficult questions about God's role in your divorce. Answer honestly but with reassurance of God's love and faithfulness.

Biblical Encouragement: Deuteronomy 6:6-7 instructs parents, "These commandments that I give you today are to be on your hearts. Impress them on your children. Talk about them when you sit at home and when you walk along the road, when you lie down and when you get up." Your role as a spiritual guide is crucial.

—-

5. Trusting God in Parenting

Parenting after divorce requires leaning heavily on God for wisdom, strength, and guidance.

Pray for Wisdom: Ask God to show you how to handle challenges, communicate effectively, and meet your children's unique needs. James 1:5 reminds us, "If any of you lacks wisdom, you should ask God, who gives generously to all without finding fault, and it will be given to you."

Rely on His Strength: There will be moments when parenting feels overwhelming. In those times, remember Philippians 4:13: "I can do all this through him who gives me strength."

—-

Practical Tips for Success

1. Create a Co-Parenting Calendar: Outline custody arrangements, school events, and extracurricular activities. This reduces confusion and promotes cooperation.

2. Encourage Open Communication: Let your children talk about their feelings and experiences without fear of judgment.

3. Seek Support: If co-parenting becomes too challenging, consider seeking help from a mediator, counselor, or pastor.

4. Model Resilience: Show your children that, with God's help, it's possible to overcome difficulties and thrive.

—-

Encouragement for the Journey

Parenting after divorce is not without its difficulties, but it's also an opportunity to grow as a parent and deepen your relationship with your children. Remember, God has entrusted these children to you, and He will equip you for the task.

As you navigate this new chapter, rely on God's guidance and lean into His promises. Trust that He is working in your family's life, even when things feel uncertain.

—-

A Closing Prayer

Heavenly Father, thank You for the gift of my children. I ask for Your wisdom and strength as I navigate parenting after divorce. Help me to love, guide, and nurture my children according to Your Word. Grant me patience and grace in co-parenting, and protect my children's hearts and minds. May they grow in their faith and know Your love. In Jesus' name, Amen.

Would you like to include tips for single parents or additional resources for children's spiritual growth in this chapter?

Chapter 7: Financial Stewardship After Divorce

Divorce often brings significant financial changes, which can feel overwhelming and unsettling. Whether you're transitioning to a single income, managing debt, or figuring out how to rebuild financially, this season requires wisdom, diligence, and trust in God's provision. Proverbs 21:5 reminds us, "The plans of the diligent lead to profit as surely as haste leads to poverty."

This chapter will guide you in handling financial upheaval, creating a plan for stability, and learning to trust God as your ultimate provider.

—-

Understanding the Financial Impact of Divorce

Divorce can disrupt finances in many ways:

Loss of a dual income.

Increased expenses (e.g., legal fees, housing changes).

Division of assets and debts.

New financial responsibilities, such as child support or alimony.

While the challenges are real, this is also an opportunity to reevaluate your financial habits, align them with biblical principles, and build a foundation for future stability.

—-

1. Trusting God as Your Provider

When financial stress feels overwhelming, it's essential to remind yourself of God's faithfulness.

God's Promise of Provision: Philippians 4:19 assures us, "And my God will meet all your needs according to the riches of his glory in Christ Jesus." Trust that God sees your needs and will provide for you.

Prayer for Guidance: Begin each day by asking God for wisdom in managing your finances and peace as you navigate uncertainty.

Cultivate Gratitude: Focus on the blessings you still have. A grateful heart shifts your perspective and helps you trust God's plan.

Reflection Activity: Write down three ways God has provided for you recently. Reflect on how His faithfulness in the past can give you confidence for the future.

—-

2. Building a Post-Divorce Budget

A realistic budget is a vital tool for financial stewardship. It helps you prioritize your needs, eliminate wasteful spending, and regain control of your finances.

Step 1: Assess Your Financial Situation:

List your income sources (e.g., salary, child support, alimony).

Document all expenses, including fixed costs (e.g., rent, utilities) and variable costs (e.g., groceries, entertainment).

Step 2: Categorize Needs vs. Wants:

Essentials: Housing, utilities, food, transportation, and insurance.

Discretionary: Subscriptions, dining out, entertainment.

Step 3: Track Your Spending:

Use tools like spreadsheets, budgeting apps, or notebooks to monitor where your money goes.

Adjust as necessary to ensure your spending aligns with your priorities.

Step 4: Build an Emergency Fund:

Aim to save 3–6 months' worth of living expenses to prepare for unexpected costs.

Biblical Principle: Proverbs 27:23 advises, "Be sure you know the condition of your flocks, give careful attention to your herds." Keeping track of your finances is an essential part of stewardship.

—-

3. Addressing Debt

If you've taken on debt during your marriage or divorce, it's important to create a plan to pay it off.

List Your Debts: Include balances, interest rates, and minimum payments.

Prioritize High-Interest Debts: Focus on paying off debts with the highest interest rates first while continuing to make minimum payments on others.

Consider a Debt Snowball Approach: Pay off smaller debts first to build momentum and confidence.

Avoid Accumulating New Debt: Live within your means and resist the temptation to rely on credit cards.

Encouragement: Romans 13:8 says, "Let no debt remain outstanding, except the continuing debt to love one another." By addressing your financial obligations diligently, you honor God and gain financial freedom.

—-

4. Seeking Wise Counsel

Financial decisions can feel daunting, especially during a season of transition. Seeking wise counsel can help you make informed and godly choices.

Meet with a Financial Advisor: A professional can help you create a comprehensive financial plan tailored to your situation.

Seek Godly Mentorship: Connect with someone in your church or faith community who has experience managing finances and can provide biblical guidance.

Take a Financial Stewardship Class: Many churches offer classes like Financial Peace University to equip you with practical tools and biblical principles.

Biblical Insight: Proverbs 15:22 states, "Plans fail for lack of counsel, but with many advisers they succeed." Don't hesitate to ask for help when needed.

—-

5. Planning for a Secure Future

Divorce doesn't just affect your present finances—it also impacts your long-term financial goals.

Reevaluate Retirement Plans: Adjust your contributions and investments to ensure a stable future.

Set New Financial Goals: These could include saving for your children's education, buying a home, or starting a business.

Educate Yourself: Learn basic financial skills, such as investing, budgeting, and tax planning, to feel more confident about your financial decisions.

—-

6. Practicing Generosity in Difficult Times

Even when finances are tight, God calls us to be generous. Giving doesn't just bless others—it strengthens your faith and reminds you of God's provision.

Tithing: Continue to give faithfully to your church as an act of worship and trust in God.

Supporting Others: Look for small ways to bless others, such as donating time or resources.

Trusting God's Promises: Luke 6:38 says, "Give, and it will be given to you. A good measure, pressed down, shaken together and running over, will be poured into your lap."

Activity: Reflect on how you can practice generosity, even in small ways, and commit to taking one step this month.

—-

Encouragement for the Journey

Rebuilding your finances after divorce takes time, effort, and trust in God. Remember, you are not alone in this journey. God is your provider, and He equips you with the wisdom and strength to steward your resources well.

While this season may feel uncertain, it's also an opportunity to build a stronger financial foundation rooted in biblical principles. By trusting God, seeking wise counsel, and planning diligently, you can experience financial stability and peace.

—-

A Closing Prayer

Heavenly Father, thank You for being my ultimate provider. In this season of financial uncertainty, I ask for Your wisdom and guidance. Help me to manage my resources faithfully and to trust in Your provision. Teach me to honor You with my finances and to live generously, even when times are challenging. Thank You for Your faithfulness and for meeting all my needs. In Jesus' name, Amen.

Would you like additional resources, such as budgeting templates or recommended books, to accompany this chapter?

Chapter 8: Guarding Your Heart and Finding Love Again

Divorce leaves emotional wounds that require time, attention, and God's grace to heal. While the idea of finding love again may feel far off—or perhaps too soon—it's crucial to approach this topic with wisdom, discernment, and a heart surrendered to God. Proverbs 4:23 reminds us, "Above all else, guard your heart, for everything you do flows from it."

This chapter focuses on healing from past relationships, redefining love through a biblical lens, and navigating new relationships with prayerful consideration.

—-

1. The Importance of Healing Before Moving Forward

Jumping into a new relationship without addressing the pain from your divorce can lead to more hurt and brokenness. Healing is a journey that allows you to process, reflect, and rediscover yourself in Christ.

Acknowledge Your Wounds: It's natural to feel anger, rejection, or fear. Give yourself permission to grieve the loss of your previous relationship.

Seek God's Healing: Psalm 147:3 says, "He heals the brokenhearted and binds up their wounds." Spend time in prayer and Scripture, inviting God into the deepest places of your pain.

Forgive Fully: Letting go of bitterness and resentment is key to healing. Forgiveness doesn't mean excusing wrongs but releasing yourself from the burden of anger.

Avoid Rebounding: Filling the void with a new relationship too soon can hinder genuine healing. Instead, focus on growing in your faith and personal development.

Reflection Activity: Write a letter to your former spouse, expressing all the emotions you've felt since the divorce. You don't need to send it—this is an exercise in releasing what's been bottled up.

—-

2. Rediscovering Biblical Love

Before considering a new relationship, take time to understand love from God's perspective.

God as the Source of Love: 1 John 4:8 reminds us, "Whoever does not love does not know God, because God is love." True love begins with a deep relationship with God.

Characteristics of Biblical Love: Reflect on 1 Corinthians 13:4-7, which describes love as patient, kind, humble, and enduring. This passage provides a blueprint for healthy, Christ-centered relationships.

Self-Love Through Christ: Recognize your worth as God's creation. Genesis 1:27 affirms that you are made in His image, which means you are valuable, loved, and deserving of respect.

Reflection Question: How does God's definition of love differ from what you've experienced in the past?

—-

3. Guarding Your Heart

Guarding your heart doesn't mean closing yourself off from love; it means being intentional and wise about whom and what you allow into your life.

Set Boundaries: Establish clear boundaries in new relationships to ensure they align with your values and respect your healing process.

Discern Red Flags: Be aware of unhealthy patterns, such as emotional dependency, dishonesty, or controlling behaviors.

Seek God's Wisdom: Pray for discernment and clarity when considering a new relationship. James 1:5 promises, "If any of you lacks wisdom, you should ask God, who gives generously to all without finding fault, and it will be given to you."

Practical Tip: Write down the qualities you desire in a future partner, ensuring they align with biblical principles. Use this list as a guide to evaluate potential relationships.

—-

4. Preparing for a New Relationship

Once you've taken time to heal and rediscovered your identity in Christ, you may feel ready to explore the possibility of love again. Approach this with caution and prayer.

Be Honest About Your Past: Share your story openly, but only when trust has been established. Transparency builds a strong foundation.

Embrace Friendship First: A healthy relationship often starts with a strong friendship. Take time to get to know the person without rushing into romantic commitments.

Evaluate Spiritual Compatibility: Ensure that your potential partner shares your faith and values. Amos 3:3 asks, "Do two walk together unless they have agreed to do so?" A shared commitment to Christ is vital for a lasting relationship.

Involve Trusted Mentors: Seek guidance from trusted friends, family, or church leaders. They can provide valuable insight and accountability.

Biblical Principle: Proverbs 19:20 advises, "Listen to advice and accept discipline, and at the end you will be counted among the wise."

—-

5. Trusting God's Timing

It's tempting to rush into a new relationship to fill the void left by divorce, but God's timing is perfect. Trust Him to lead you to the right person at the right time.

Practice Patience: Psalm 27:14 encourages us, "Wait for the Lord; be strong and take heart and wait for the Lord." Use this waiting period to deepen your relationship with God.

Let God Write Your Love Story: Surrender your desire for a relationship to God, trusting Him to bring the right person into your life.

Find Contentment in Singleness: Embrace this season as an opportunity for personal growth, ministry, and discovering new passions.

Activity: Make a list of ways you can serve God and others during this season of singleness.

—-

6. When Love Finds You Again

If you meet someone who aligns with your values and faith, approach the relationship with intention and prayer.

Commit to Purity: Uphold biblical principles in your relationship, honoring God with your actions. 1 Thessalonians 4:7 reminds us, "For God did not call us to be impure, but to live a holy life."

Build Together Spiritually: Pray together, attend church, and study Scripture as a couple to strengthen your bond in Christ.

Seek Premarital Counseling: If the relationship progresses toward marriage, consider premarital counseling to address potential challenges and build a strong foundation.

—-

Encouragement for the Journey

Finding love again is a beautiful possibility, but it begins with healing, self-discovery, and trusting God's plan. Whether you remain single or enter a new relationship, your ultimate fulfillment comes from Christ, not another person.

God is with you in this journey, guiding your steps and preparing your heart for the future He has in store. Trust Him to lead you toward a life of joy, purpose, and, if it's His will, a Christ-centered partnership.

—-

A Closing Prayer

Heavenly Father, thank You for Your love, which is perfect and unwavering. As I heal from past relationships, help me to guard my heart and seek Your will in all things. Prepare me for the future You have planned, whether that includes singleness or a new relationship. Grant me wisdom, patience, and discernment as I navigate this journey. Above all, let my life reflect Your love and glory. In Jesus' name, Amen.

Would you like additional discussion questions or reflection prompts to help readers apply the principles in this chapter?

Chapter 9: Living with Purpose

Divorce can feel like a loss of purpose, an event that shatters dreams and leaves you with a sense of aimlessness. However, as a believer, you are never without purpose. Your life is in the hands of a sovereign God who works all things—even the painful experiences—together for good. Romans 8:28 assures us, "And we know that in all things God works for the good of those who love him, who have been called according to his purpose."

In this chapter, we explore how to use your experiences after divorce not only to heal but also to glorify God, inspire others, and step boldly into a life of purpose. Your story can become a testimony of God's faithfulness and a source of encouragement for others walking a similar journey.

—-

1. Embracing God's Purpose for Your Life

No matter the circumstances, God has a plan for you. Divorce may have shifted your path, but it hasn't canceled your calling. It's important to seek God's will in this new season of life, understanding that He has work for you to do.

Understand Your Identity in Christ: Remember that you are His beloved child, made for good works. Ephesians 2:10 says, "For we are God's handiwork, created in Christ Jesus to do good works, which God prepared in advance for us to do." Your divorce does not disqualify you from serving God; instead, it equips you with a deeper compassion and understanding to reach others.

Seek God's Guidance: Ask God to reveal His purpose for you in this season. Jeremiah 29:11 reminds us of God's loving plans: "For I know the plans I have for you," declares the Lord, "plans to prosper you and not to harm you, plans to give you a hope and a future." Trust that God will guide you into fulfilling your purpose, even if it looks different from what you expected.

Reflection Activity: Spend time in prayer and ask God, "What is Your purpose for me in this season? How can I serve You with my life?" Journal the thoughts that come to mind.

—-

2. Using Your Story to Inspire Others

One of the most powerful ways to live with purpose is by sharing your story. Your journey through divorce—how you've faced the pain, found healing, and leaned into God—can be an inspiration to others.

Be Open About Your Journey: While it may feel vulnerable, sharing your story with others who are struggling can be a source of great encouragement. God often uses our weaknesses to reveal His strength.

Offer Hope: Your testimony can be a beacon of hope for someone who feels like they're in the dark. Let others know that healing is possible, and that God can redeem even the most painful circumstances.

Use Social Media or Blogs: Consider writing articles or sharing on social media about your journey, how God has worked in your life, and how He has sustained you.

Join Support Groups: Leading or joining support groups for those going through divorce or broken relationships can help you both heal and give back.

Biblical Example: The Samaritan woman at the well (John 4:1-30) shared her encounter with Jesus, leading many to believe in Him. Your story, when shared with humility and grace, can have a similar impact on others.

—-

3. Volunteering: Serving Others in Their Pain

When we serve others, we reflect the heart of Christ. Volunteering is a way to redirect your focus outward and find healing through helping others.

Serve at Your Church: There are always opportunities to serve, whether it's through teaching, providing meals, or supporting church events. When we give our time to others, we cultivate a heart of compassion and build connections.

Volunteer at a Women's Shelter or Divorce Support Group: If you've walked through divorce, you understand the pain and challenges. You can use your experience to minister to others by volunteering at shelters, counseling services, or divorce recovery programs.

Serve the Elderly or Vulnerable: Many times, we forget that God calls us to serve those who are most vulnerable, such as the elderly or children in need. Giving back can help restore a sense of purpose and perspective.

Volunteer to Mentor: If you've found healing, consider mentoring someone who is navigating divorce, single parenthood, or emotional recovery. Sharing your wisdom can help others avoid common pitfalls and find encouragement along the way.

Biblical Principle: 1 Peter 4:10 says, "Each of you should use whatever gift you have received to serve others, as faithful stewards of God's grace in its various forms." Your unique gifts and experiences can be used to bless others in powerful ways.

—-

4. Discovering and Pursuing New Passions

Divorce can free you from the distractions and limitations of the past, allowing you to discover new passions and interests that align with God's will for your life.

Invest in Personal Growth: Now is the time to explore new interests—whether it's taking up a new hobby, learning a skill, or finishing an education you previously set aside. Pursuing your God-given potential helps you live a life of fulfillment.

Get Involved in New Ministry Areas: Perhaps you've always wanted to serve in a new capacity in your church or community. Now is the time to explore opportunities that align with your heart and talents.

Travel or Explore New Areas of Interest: God may open doors for you to explore new parts of the world, or even your local community, that will enrich your life and deepen your understanding of His creation.

Biblical Encouragement: Ecclesiastes 3:1 states, "There is a time for everything, and a season for every activity under the heavens." Trust that God is leading you to the right opportunities for growth and service in this new season.

—-

5. Cultivating a Lifestyle of Prayer and Discernment

As you move forward in finding purpose after divorce, it's essential to maintain a life rooted in prayer and discernment. When you are closely connected to God through prayer, He will reveal His plan and direction for your life.

Pray for Clarity: Pray regularly for guidance and clarity on how to live with purpose. Trust that God will give you direction in His time.

Seek God's Will in All Things: Proverbs 3:5-6 instructs us, "Trust in the Lord with all your heart and lean not on your own understanding; in all your ways submit to him, and he will make your paths straight." God's plan is always better than our own, and we can trust Him to direct our steps.

Embrace God's Timing: Understand that God's plan may take time to unfold. Be patient and faithful in the waiting, knowing that He is at work in every part of your journey.

—-

6. Living a Legacy of Purpose

Finally, living with purpose means being intentional about the legacy you want to leave. You may not be able to control everything, but you can choose to live in a way that honors God, strengthens your faith, and blesses those around you.

Leave a Legacy of Faith: Invest in your children's spiritual growth, mentor younger believers, and serve in your community. Leave a legacy of wisdom, love, and Christ-centered living.

Be a Light in Your Community: Your actions, your words, and your love for others can impact many. Live intentionally, reflecting the love of Christ in everything you do.

Biblical Example: In Acts 9, the life of Dorcas (Tabitha) is remembered for her good works and acts of charity. Her legacy was one of kindness, compassion, and service to others. May your life be marked by similar attributes.

—-

A Closing Prayer

Heavenly Father, thank You for the purpose You have placed in my life, even in the aftermath of divorce. Help me to trust You fully as I seek to use my story, my experiences, and my gifts to serve You and others. Lead me to the places and people where I can be a light for Your Kingdom. I pray that I would live a life of purpose, guided by Your wisdom and love. In Jesus' name, Amen.

—-

Reflection Prompt: What passions or areas of service do you feel God calling you to explore in this season of your life? How can you begin living with purpose today?

Would you like additional resources on how to serve others or further explore purpose-driven living?

Chapter 10: A New Beginning

Divorce may feel like an end, but in God's economy, it is often the beginning of something new. This chapter invites you to step forward into the future with faith, hope, and courage, trusting that God has a plan for your life that is even greater than you can imagine. Isaiah 43:19 declares, "See, I am doing a new thing! Now it springs up; do you not perceive it?" This is a powerful reminder that God's work in your life is not bound by your past. In fact, the future He has for you may be more beautiful and fulfilling than you could have ever envisioned.

As you journey through this new chapter, it's essential to embrace it with an open heart, knowing that God's plans are always for your good. You can take confident steps forward, trusting that He will walk with you every step of the way.

—

1. Trusting God's Plan for Your Future

The path to healing and wholeness after divorce may seem uncertain, but one thing remains sure: God has a plan for you. Trusting in God's sovereignty is the key to finding peace and joy in the future.

God's Plan is for Good: Jeremiah 29:11 reminds us, "For I know the plans I have for you," declares the Lord, "plans to prosper you and not to harm you, plans to give you a hope and a future." Divorce might have altered the trajectory of your life, but God is still at work, weaving your story for good. He promises to lead you into a future filled with hope.

Let Go of Control: The temptation to control your future is strong, but surrendering to God's will brings true peace. Trusting Him means believing that His timing and direction are perfect, even when it's hard to see. Proverbs 3:5-6 encourages us, "Trust in the Lord with all your heart and lean not on your own understanding; in all your ways submit to Him, and He will make your paths straight."

God is the Author of New Beginnings: Just as God created the world anew each morning, He is constantly renewing and restoring your life. Embrace the concept that every new day is an opportunity for transformation.

Reflection Activity: Take a moment to pray and ask God to reveal His purpose for your life in this season. Write down any thoughts, verses, or feelings He brings to mind.

—-

2. Celebrating Progress, Not Perfection

The road to healing after divorce is not linear. There will be setbacks, but it's important to celebrate the small victories along the way. Healing takes time, and each step forward, no matter how small, is an evidence of God's grace in your life.

Recognize Your Growth: Reflect on how far you've come since the divorce. Perhaps you've found peace where there was once turmoil, or you've begun to establish a new routine. Acknowledge these moments as signs of progress.

Celebrate Your Strength: Even on the days when you feel weak, remember that you are stronger than you think. God has been faithful to carry you through the darkest moments. Celebrate the fact that you've made it through the storm, and now you stand on the other side.

Embrace Imperfection: Healing is not about achieving perfection; it's about progress. Philippians 1:6 assures us, "Being confident of this, that he who began a good work in you will carry it on to completion until the day of Christ Jesus." God is working in you, and He will continue His work until it's finished.

Reflection Activity: Write a letter to yourself celebrating how far you've come. Acknowledge the ways you've grown and the strengths you've discovered in yourself through this journey.

—-

3. Stepping Into the Future with Faith and Courage

It's normal to feel a sense of fear when facing the unknown future, but God has not given you a spirit of fear, but of power, love, and a sound mind (2 Timothy 1:7). Stepping forward in faith means facing each day with courage, trusting that God will guide you into the future He has prepared for you.

Step Boldly: Moving forward requires courage, but with God on your side, you can step into this new season with boldness. Joshua 1:9 encourages us, "Be strong and courageous. Do not be afraid; do not be discouraged, for the Lord your God will be with you wherever you go."

Don't Let Fear Hold You Back: While fear may try to creep in, you can choose to move forward despite it. Trust in God's strength to face new challenges and opportunities.

Take Faith-Filled Action: Whether it's pursuing a new job, ministry, or relationship, take steps in faith, knowing that God will direct your path. Isaiah 30:21 says, "Whether you turn to the right or to the left, your ears will hear a voice behind you, saying, 'This is the way; walk in it.'" Trust that God is guiding your every move.

Reflection Question: What areas of your life require you to step out in faith? How can you move forward with courage, knowing God is with you?

—-

4. Leaning on God's Promises

As you face the future, cling to the promises God has made to you in His Word. These promises are the foundation on which you can build a life of confidence and hope.

God Promises to Provide: Whatever you need, God promises to provide. Philippians 4:19 says, "And my God will meet all your needs according to the riches of his glory in Christ Jesus." Trust that He will supply what you need—emotionally, spiritually, financially.

God Promises Peace: The journey after divorce can often feel like turmoil, but God promises peace. John 14:27 says, "Peace I leave with you; my peace I give you. I do not give to you as the world gives. Do not let your hearts be troubled and do not be afraid." Lean into His peace as you move forward.

God Promises His Presence: You are never alone. God is with you every step of the way. Isaiah 41:10 reassures us, "So do not fear, for I am with you; do not be dismayed, for I am your God. I will strengthen you and help you; I will uphold you with my righteous right hand."

Activity: Write down five promises from Scripture that resonate with your current situation. Whenever you face doubts, revisit these promises and remind yourself of God's faithfulness.

—-

5. Walking in New Freedom

Divorce often carries feelings of shame, regret, or a sense of defeat. However, through Christ, you are free. You are free from guilt, shame, and condemnation. Embrace this freedom as a fresh start and a new identity in Christ.

Live in Your New Identity: You are no longer defined by your past, mistakes, or the divorce itself. 2 Corinthians 5:17 says, "Therefore, if anyone is in Christ, the new creation has come: The old has gone, the new is here!" Walk in the freedom of your new identity in Christ.

Embrace the New You: Divorce has shaped you, but it does not define you. You are a new creation, and with that comes a new opportunity to live the life God has called you to.

Celebrate the Gift of Freedom: The future is full of new opportunities. Walk in the freedom that Christ has given you, unburdened by the past.

Reflection Activity: Create a vision board or journal about the freedom you have in Christ. Let it represent the new life you are walking into.

—-

6. Moving Forward with Hope

The future is bright when you trust in God's promises. As you face each day, do so with the expectation that God is leading you into a new season filled with His goodness.

Hope Anchors the Soul: Hebrews 6:19 says, "We have this hope as an anchor for the soul, firm and secure." Your hope in Christ will anchor you during the storms and keep you moving forward with confidence.

Expect New Beginnings: Believe that God is already at work in your future, even when you cannot yet see it. Isaiah 43:19 reminds us, "See, I am doing a new thing! Now it springs up; do you not perceive it?" Trust that God's work in you is far from over.

—-

A Closing Prayer

Heavenly Father, thank You for the new beginnings You are doing in my life. I trust in Your plan and Your promises. Help me to embrace the future with faith, courage, and hope. Thank You for walking with me through the storms, and for leading me into a new season filled with Your peace and purpose. I lean on Your grace, knowing that You will continue to work all things together for my good. In Jesus' name, Amen.

—-

Reflection Question: What new beginnings are you excited to embrace? How can you cultivate faith, hope, and courage as you step into the future?

Conclusion: A Journey Worth Taking

As we come to the close of this journey through "Life After Divorce," I want to remind you that healing, growth, and reliance on God are not just abstract concepts—they are the practical steps to building a new, vibrant life after a challenging chapter. Divorce may feel like the end of one story, but as we've explored together, it is also the beginning of a fresh and transformative journey.

You are not defined by your past, your pain, or your mistakes. God has a future for you that is filled with hope, purpose, and restoration. Each chapter of this book has guided you to recognize that healing is not just about recovering from what you've lost but embracing what God wants to do in and through your life. It's about rediscovering your true identity in Christ, rebuilding your faith, and learning to forgive—both others and yourself. It's about navigating the challenges of loneliness, co-parenting, and finances, while remaining rooted in biblical truths and His promises.

Your life after divorce can be rich, fulfilling, and full of potential when you put your trust in God's plan. Through prayer, scripture, community, and the strength of His Holy Spirit, you have everything you need to move forward in faith.

—-

Recap: Key Themes

1. Healing is a Process: It's okay to grieve, but remember that healing is possible. Take time to grieve but don't remain stuck in despair.

2. Growth in Christ: Through every challenge, God is shaping you into a stronger and more faithful person. Let your struggles refine you, not define you.

3. Reliance on God: You are not alone. Every step forward is sustained by His strength. Lean into God's promises and trust His plan for your future.

—-

Final Scripture: A Blessing for You

As you move forward, let this scripture be a reminder of God's continued presence in your life. May these words bring peace and encouragement as you step into the future with faith and courage.

"The Lord bless you and keep you; the Lord make his face shine on you and be gracious to you; the Lord turn his face toward you and give you peace." (Numbers 6:24-25)

—-

Call to Action: Keep Moving Forward

The journey does not end with these pages. In fact, it is just the beginning. You are stepping into a future full of opportunities to glorify God and live out the fullness of His plan for you. No matter where you are on this journey, remember that each day is a new chance to seek God's will, trust in His provision, and live with purpose.

Keep moving forward with courage. As you seek God in every step, trust that He is guiding you, providing for you, and making all things new. Your story is far from over, and with God's help, the best chapters are yet to come.

—-

Final Prayer:

Father, thank You for bringing me through this journey of healing and restoration. Help me to continue walking in Your light, trusting in Your plan, and seeking Your will for every step of my life. I surrender my past to You and embrace the future with hope, knowing that You are with me. Thank You for Your love, Your grace, and Your faithfulness. In Jesus' name, Amen.

May you continue to find strength, peace, and joy in this new chapter of your life. Trust that God is with you, guiding you toward a future filled with His blessings and purpose.

For permission requests, contact:

Tawanda Tawanda

[skiesonlinemedia@gmail.com]]

Printed in [Africa]

—-

Disclaimer

The content of this book is intended for informational and inspirational purposes only. The author and publisher have made every effort to ensure the accuracy of the information provided, but they do not guarantee the completeness or effectiveness of the advice. Readers are encouraged to seek professional counsel for personal matters and concerns related to divorce, mental health, or other significant life changes.

www.ingramcontent.com/pod-product-compliance
Lightning Source LLC
LaVergne TN
LVHW040954150826
845672LV00002B/689

* 9 7 9 8 2 3 0 1 4 1 6 3 1 *